Paul Bunyan

an operetta in two acts
and a prologue

Libretto by
W. H. AUDEN

Set to music by
BENJAMIN BRITTEN
Op. 17

FABER *ff* MUSIC

Libretto © 1976 by Faber Music Ltd
First published in 1976 by Faber Music Ltd
This amended edition first published in 1999
by Faber Music Ltd, 3 Queen Square, London, WC1N 3AU
Cover illustration from the poster for the first production
Printed in England by Halstan & Co Ltd

ISBN 0 571 51938 5

Also available on sale from the publishers:
Vocal Score (0 571 50538 4)
Ballads from *Paul Bunyan* for medium voice and piano or guitar (0 571 50653 4)

The first performance of *Paul Bunyan* was given by the Columbia Theater Associates of Columbia University, New York, with the co-operation of the Columbia University Department of Music and a Chorus from the New York Schola Cantorum, conducted by Hugh Ross, in Brander Matthews Hall on 5 May 1941.

To buy Faber Music publications
or to find out about the full range of titles available
please contact your local music retailer or Faber Music sales enquiries:

Tel: +44 (0) 171 833 7931
Fax: +44 (0) 171 833 7930
E-mail: sales@fabermusic.co.uk
Website: www.fabermusic.co.uk

CHARACTERS

CHORUS of OLD TREES	SATB	
FOUR YOUNG TREES	SSTT	In the Prologue
THREE WILD GEESE	MS.MS.S	

NARRATOR	Baritone or Tenor	In the Ballad Interludes

VOICE of PAUL BUNYAN	Spoken part
JOHNNY INKSLINGER, bookkeeper	Tenor
TINY, daughter of PAUL BUNYAN	Soprano
HOT BISCUIT SLIM, a good cook	Tenor
SAM SHARKEY } two bad cooks	Tenor
BEN BENNY	Bass
HEL HELSON, foreman	Baritone
ANDY ANDERSON	Tenor
PETE PETERSON	Tenor
JEN JENSON } four Swedes	Bass
CROSS CROSSHAULSON	Bass
JOHN SHEARS, a farmer	Baritone
WESTERN UNION BOY	Tenor
FIDO, a dog	High soprano
MOPPET } two cats	Mezzo-soprano
POPPET	Mezzo-soprano
QUARTET of the DEFEATED	Alto, Tenor, Baritone, Bass
FOUR CRONIES of HEL HELSON	Four Baritones
HERON, MOON, WIND, BEETLE, SQUIRREL	Spoken parts

Chorus of LUMBERJACKS, FARMERS and FRONTIER WOMEN

Paul Bunyan

No. 1 Introduction

No. 2 Prologue
In the forest

CHORUS of OLD TREES

Since the birth
Of the earth
Time has gone
On and on:
Rivers saunter,
Rivers run,
Till they enter
The enormous level sea,
Where they prefer to be.

But the sun
Is too hot,
And will not
Let alone
Waves glad-handed,
Lazy crowd,
Educates them
Till they change into a cloud,
But can't control them long.

For the will
Just to fall
Is too strong
In them all;
Revolution
Turns to rain
Whence more solid
Sensible Creatures gain:
In falling they serve life.

Here are we
Flower and tree,
Green, alive,
Glad to be,
And our proper
Places know:
Winds and waters
Travel; we remain and grow;
We like life to be slow.

5

FOUR YOUNG TREES

No. No. No. No.

CHORUS of OLD TREES

O.

FOUR YOUNG TREES

We do *Not* want life to be slow.

CHORUS of OLD TREES

Reds.

FOUR YOUNG TREES

We are *bored* with standing still,
We want to see things and go places.

CHORUS of OLD TREES

Such nonsense. It's only a phase.
They're sick. They're crazy.

(*Enter* TWO WILD GEESE.)

TWO WILD GEESE

Ooh!
O how terrible to be
As old-fashioned as a tree:
Dull old stick that won't go out;
What on earth do they talk about?
 Unexpressive,
 Unprogressive,
Unsophisticated lout.
How can pines or grass or sage
Understand the Modern Age?

(*Enter* THIRD WILD GOOSE.)

Ooh!
What's up, eh? Do tell us, quick!

THREE WILD GEESE

That's the best I ever heard!
Shall we tell them? Now?
You are all to leave here.

CHORUS of OLD TREES

What?
It's a lie!

6

Hurrah!

CHORUS of OLD TREES

Don't listen!

FOUR YOUNG TREES

How?

THREE WILD GEESE

Far away from here
A mission will find a performer.

CHORUS of OLD TREES

A mission?
What mission?

THREE WILD GEESE

To bring you to another life.

FOUR YOUNG TREES

What kind of performer?

THREE WILD GEESE

A Man.

FOUR YOUNG TREES

What is a man?

CHORUS of OLD TREES

What is a man?

THREE WILD GEESE

A man is a form of life
That dreams in order to act
And acts in order to dream
And has a name of his own.

FOUR YOUNG TREES and CHORUS of OLD TREES

What is this name?

THREE WILD GEESE

Paul Bunyan.

CHORUS of OLD TREES

How silly.

FOUR YOUNG TREES

When are we to see him?

THREE WILD GEESE

He will be born at the next Blue Moon.

CHORUS of OLD TREES

It isn't true,
I'm so frightened.
Don't worry.
There won't be a Blue Moon in our lifetime.
Don't say that. It's unlucky.

(*The moon begins to turn blue.*)

FOUR YOUNG TREES

Look at the moon! It's turning blue.

CHORUS of OLD TREES

Look at the moon! It's turning blue.

THREE WILD GEESE

It isn't very often the conservatives are wrong,
Tomorrow normally is only yesterday again,
Society is right in saying nine times out of ten
Respectability's enough to carry one along.

CHORUS of OLD TREES

But once in a while the odd thing happens,
   Once in a while the dream comes true,
And the whole pattern of life is altered,
   Once in a while the moon turns blue.

SEMI-CHORUS of OLD TREES

We can't pretend we like it, that it's what we'd choose,
But what's the point in fussing when one can't refuse
And nothing is as bad as one thinks it will be,
The children look so happy – Well, well, we shall see.

FOUR YOUNG TREES

I want to be a vessel sailing on the sea,
I want to be a roof with houses under me,
I've always longed for edges, and I'd love to be a square.
How swell to be a dado and how swell to be a chair.

TUTTI

But once in a while the odd thing happens,
   Once in a while the dream comes true,
And the whole pattern of life is altered,
   Once in a while the moon turns blue.

8

No. 2a First Ballad Interlude

The cold wind blew through the crooked thorn,
Up in the North a boy was born.

His hair was black, his eyes were blue,
His mouth turned up at the corners too.

A fairy stood beside his bed;
'You shall never, never grow old,' she said,

'Paul Bunyan is to be your name';
Then she departed whence she came.

You must believe me when I say,
He grew six inches every day.

You must believe me when I speak,
He gained three–four–six pounds every week.

He grew so fast, by the time he was eight,
He was as tall as the Empire State.

The length of his stride's a historical fact;
Three point seven miles to be exact.

When he ordered a jacket, the New England mills
For months had no more unemployment ills.

When he wanted a snapshot to send to his friends,
They found they had to use a telephoto lens.

But let me tell you in advance,
His dreams were of greater significance.

His favourite dream was of felling trees,
A fancy which grew by swift degrees.

One night he dreamt he was to be
The greatest logger in history.

He woke to feel something stroking his brow,
And found it was the tongue of an enormous cow.

From horn to horn or from lug to lug,
Was forty-seven axe-heads and a baccy plug.

But what would have most bewildered you
Was the colour of her hide which was bright bright blue.

But Bunyan wasn't surprised at all;
Said, 'I'll call you Babe, you call me Paul.'

He pointed to a meadow, said, 'Take a bite:
For you're leaving with me for the South tonight.'

Over the mountains, across the streams
They went to find Paul Bunyan's dreams.

The bear and the beaver waved a paw,
The magpie chattered, the squirrel swore.

The trappers ran out from their lonely huts
Scratching their heads with their rifle butts.

For a year and a day they travelled fast.
'This is the place', Paul said at last.

The forest stretched for miles around,
The sound of their breathing was the only sound.

Paul picked a pine-tree and scratched his shins,
Said, 'This is the place where our work begins.'

ACT ONE

Scene 1
A clearing in the forest

No. 3 Bunyan's Greeting

VOICE of PAUL BUNYAN
It is a spring morning without benefit of young persons.
It is a sky that has never registered weeping or rebellion.
It is a forest full of innocent beasts. There are none who blush at the memory of an
    ancient folly, none who hide beneath dyed fabrics a malicious heart.
It is America, but not yet.
Wanted. Disturbers of public order, men without foresight or fear.
Wanted. Energetic madmen. Those who have thought themselves a body large
    enough to devour their dreams.
Wanted. The lost. Those indestructibles whom defeat can never change. Poets of the
    bottle, clergymen of a ridiculous gospel, actors who should have been engineers
    and lawyers who should have been sea-captains, saints of circumstance,
    desperados, unsuccessful wanderers, all who can hear the invitation of the earth,
    America, youngest of her daughters, awaits the barbarians of marriage.

No. 3a Call of Lumberjacks

CHORUS of LUMBERJACKS

(*Starting offstage and gradually approaching.*)

Down the Line. Timber–rrr.

No. 4 Lumberjacks' Chorus

LUMBERJACK 1

My birthplace was in Sweden, it's a very long way off,
My appetite was hearty but I couldn't get enough;
When suddenly I heard a roar across the wide blue sea,
'I'll give you steak and onions if you'll come and work for me.'

CHORUS of LUMBERJACKS

We rise at dawn of day,
We're handsome, free and gay,
   We're lumberjacks
   With saw and axe
Who are melting the forests away.

LUMBERJACK 2

In France I wooed a maiden with an alabaster skin,
But she left me for a fancy chap who played the violin;
When just about to drown myself a voice came from the sky,
'There's no one like a shanty boy to catch a maiden's eye.'

CHORUS of LUMBERJACKS

We rise at dawn, etc.

LUMBERJACK 3

Oh, long ago in Germany when sitting at my ease,
There came a knocking at the door and it was the police;
I tiptoed down the backstairs and a voice to me did say,
'There's freedom in the forests out in North Americay.'

CHORUS of LUMBERJACKS

We rise at dawn, etc.

LUMBERJACK 4

In Piccadilly Circus I stood waiting for a bus,
I thought I heard the pigeons say, 'Please run away with us';
To a land of opportunity with work and food for all,
Especially for shanty boys in Winter and in Fall.

CHORUS of LUMBERJACKS
We rise at dawn, etc.

No. 4a Bunyan's Welcome

VOICE of PAUL BUNYAN
Welcome and sit down, we have no time to waste.
The trees are waiting for the axe and we must all make haste.
So who shall be the foreman to set in hand the work
To organize the logging and see men do not shirk?

No. 5 Quartet of Swedes

FOUR SWEDES

I.

   I.

      I.

         I.

CHORUS of LUMBERJACKS: Why?

FOUR SWEDES
Swedish born and Swedish bred,
Strong in the arm and dull in the head.
Who can ever kill a Swede?
His skull is very thick indeed,
But once you get an idea in,
You'll never get it out again.

VOICE of PAUL BUNYAN: What are your names?

FOUR SWEDES
Cross Crosshaulson.
Jen Jenson.
Pete Peterson.
Andy Anderson.

VOICE of PAUL BUNYAN
In your opinion which of you, which one would be the best
To be the leader of the few and govern all the rest?

FOUR SWEDES
(*Fighting.*)

Why?
Who?
You?

12

Oh!
No, me!
Oh, he!
Yah!
Bah!

VOICE of PAUL BUNYAN: None of you, it seems, will do. We must find another.
CHORUS of LUMBERJACKS: Yes, but who?

(*Enter a* WESTERN UNION BOY, *on a bicycle.*)

WESTERN UNION BOY
A telegram, a telegram,
    A telegram from oversea.
Paul Bunyan is the name
    Of the addressee.

(*Exit across stage.*)

CHORUS of LUMBERJACKS: Bad News? Good News? Tell us what you're reading.

VOICE of PAUL BUNYAN: I have a message that will please you from the King of
    Sweden.
(*Reads:*) Dear Paul,
I hear you are looking for a head-foreman, so I'm sending you the finest logger
in my kingdom, Hel Helson. He doesn't talk much. Wishing you every success.
    Yours sincerely,
    Nel Nelson. King.

(*Enter while he is reading* HEL HELSON.)

Are you Hel Helson?
HEL HELSON: Aye tank so.
VOICE of PAUL BUNYAN: Do you know all about logging?
HEL HELSON: Aye tank so.
VOICE of PAUL BUNYAN: Are you prepared to be my head-foreman?
HEL HELSON: Aye tank so.
VOICE of PAUL BUNYAN: Then I think so too.
Now for one to cook or bake
Flapjacks, cookies, fish, or steak.

(*Enter* SAM SHARKEY *and* BEN BENNY.)

SAM SHARKEY: Sam Sharkey at your service.
BEN BENNY: Ben Benny at your service.

No. 7 Cooks' Duet

SAM SHARKEY
Sam for soups.

BEN BENNY
Ben for beans.

SAM SHARKEY
Soups feed you.

BEN BENNY
Beans for vitamins.

SAM SHARKEY
Soups satisfy,
Soups gratify.

BEN BENNY
Ten beans a day
Cure food delay.

SAM SHARKEY
Soups that nourish,
Make hope flourish,

BEN BENNY
Beans for nutrition,
Beans for ambition,

SAM SHARKEY
The Best People are crazy about soups!

BEN BENNY
Beans are all the rage among the Higher Income Groups!

SAM SHARKEY
Do you feel a left-out at parties,
when it comes to promotion are you passed over,
and does your wife talk in her sleep?
Then ask our nearest agent
to tell you about soups for success!

BEN BENNY
You owe it to yourself to learn about Beans, and how this delicious
food is the sure way to the Body Beautiful.
We will mail you a fascinating booklet

'Beans for Beauty' by return of post
if you'll send us your address.

(*Enter* JOHNNY INKSLINGER.)

INKSLINGER: Did I hear anyone say something about food?
SAM SHARKEY: What about a delicious bowl of soup?
BEN BENNY: What would you say to a nice big plate of beans?
INKSLINGER: I'll have a double portion of both, please.

(*Exeunt* SAM SHARKEY *and* BEN BENNY.)

VOICE of PAUL BUNYAN: Good-day stranger. What's your name?
INKSLINGER: Johnny Inkslinger.
VOICE of PAUL BUNYAN: Can you read?
INKSLINGER: Think of a language and I'll write you its dictionary.
VOICE of PAUL BUNYAN: Can you handle figures?
INKSLINGER: Think of an irrational number and I'll double it.
VOICE of PAUL BUNYAN
You're just the man I hoped to find
For I have large accounts to mind.
INKSLINGER: Sorry I'm busy.
VOICE of PAUL BUNYAN: What's your job?
INKSLINGER: Oh, just looking around.
VOICE of PAUL BUNYAN: Who do you work for?
INKSLINGER: Myself, silly. This is a free country.

(COOKS *enter*.)

Excuse me.
SAM SHARKEY: Your soup.
BEN BENNY: Your beans.
BOTH: Just taste them.
VOICE of PAUL BUNYAN: Wait a minute.

(COOKS *stand back.*)

Have you any money?
INKSLINGER: Search me.
VOICE of PAUL BUNYAN: How are you going to pay for your supper?
INKSLINGER: Dunno. Never thought of it.
VOICE of PAUL BUNYAN
If you work for me
You shall eat splendidly
But no work, no pay.
INKSLINGER: No sale. Good-day.

(*Exit* INKSLINGER.)

CHORUS of LUMBERJACKS
Now what on earth are we to do
For I can't keep accounts, can you?
VOICE of PAUL BUNYAN
Don't worry, he'll come back,
He has to feed.
Now what else do we lack,
Who else do we need?
SAM SHARKEY
I'd like a dog to lick up all the crumbs
And chase away the salesmen and all the drunken bums.
BEN BENNY
I'd like a pair of cats
To catch the mice and rats.

(PAUL BUNYAN *whistles – enter* FIDO, MOPPET *and* POPPET.)

No. 8 Animal Trio

FIDO

Ah!

MOPPET and POPPET

Miaou!

FIDO

The single creature lives a partial life,
Man by his eye and by his nose the hound;
He needs the deep emotions I can give,
Through him I sense a vaster hunting-ground.

MOPPET and POPPET

Like draws to like, to share is to relieve,
And sympathy the root bears love the flower;
He feels in us, and we in him perceive
A common passion for the lonely hour.

FIDO

In all his walks I follow at his side,
His faithful servant and his loving shade;

MOPPET and POPPET

We move in our apartness and our pride
About the decent dwellings he has made.

16

No. 8a Bunyan's Goodnight (i)

VOICE of PAUL BUNYAN
Off to supper and to bed,
For all our future lies ahead,
And our work must be begun
At the rising of the sun.

(*Exeunt.*)

No. 8b Exit of Lumberjacks

CHORUS of LUMBERJACKS
Down the line. Timber–rr.

No. 9 The Blues: Quartet of Defeated

VOICE of PAUL BUNYAN
Now at the beginning
To those who pause on the frontiers of an untravelled empire
Standing in empty dusk upon the eve of a tremendous task, to you all
A dream of warning.

TENOR SOLO
Gold in the North came the blizzard to say,
I left my sweetheart at the break of day,
The gold ran out and my love grew grey.
You don't know all, sir, you don't know all.

BASS SOLO
The West, said the sun, for enterprise,
A bullet in Frisco put me wise,
My last words were, 'God damn your eyes!'
You don't know all, sir, you don't know all.

ALTO SOLO
In Alabama my heart was full,
Down to the river bank I stole,
The waters of grief went over my soul.
You don't know all, sir, you don't know all.

BARITONE SOLO
In the streets of New York I was young and well,
I rode the market, the market fell,
One morning I found myself in hell.
I didn't know all, sir, I didn't know all.

ALL
We didn't know all, sir, we didn't know all.

BARITONE SOLO
In the saloons I heaved a sigh.

TENOR SOLO
Lost in deserts of alkali I lay down to die.

ALTO SOLO
There's always a sorrow can get you down.

BASS SOLO
All the world's whiskey can never drown.

ALL
You don't know all, sir, you don't know all.

ALTO SOLO
Some think they're strong, some think they're smart,
Like butterflies they're pulled apart,

ALL
America can break your heart.
You don't know all, sir, you don't know all.

(*Enter* INKSLINGER.)

VOICE of PAUL BUNYAN: Hello Mr Inkslinger. Lost anything?
INKSLINGER: I want my supper.
VOICE of PAUL BUNYAN: What about my little proposition?
INKSLINGER: You win. I'll take it. Now where's the kitchen, Mr Bunyan?
VOICE of PAUL BUNYAN: Call me Paul.
INKSLINGER: No. You're stronger than I, so I must do what you ask. But I'm not
going to pretend to like you. Good night.

(*Exit* INKSLINGER.)

No. 10 Bunyan's Goodnight (ii)

VOICE of PAUL BUNYAN
Good night, Johnny, and good luck.

No. 10a Second Ballad Interlude

NARRATOR
The Spring came and the Summer and Fall;
Paul Bunyan sat in his binnacle.

18

Regarding like a lighthouse lamp
The work going on in the lumber camps.

Dreaming dreams which now and then
He liked to tell to his lumbermen.

His phrases rolled like waves on a beach
And during the course of a single speech

Young boys grew up and needed a shave,
Old men got worried they'd be late for the grave.

He woke one morning feeling unwell,
Said to Babe: 'What's the matter? I feel like Hell.'

Babe cocked her head, said: 'Get a wife;
One can have too much of the bachelor life.'

And so one morning in the month of May
Paul went wife-hunting at the break of day.

He kept a sharp look-out, but all
The girls he saw were much too small.

But at last he came to a valley green
With mountains beside and a river between,

And there on the bank before his eyes
He beheld a girl of the proper size.

The average man if he walked in haste
Would have taken a week to get round her waist.

When you looked at her bosom you couldn't fail
To see it was built on a generous scale.

They eyed each other for an interval;
Then she said, 'I'm Carrie' and he said, 'I'm Paul.'

What happened then I've no idea,
They never told me and I wasn't there.

But whatever it was she became his wife
And they started in on the married life.

And in a year a daughter came,
Tiny she was and Tiny her name.

I wish I could say that Carrie and Paul
Were a happy pair but they weren't at all.

It's not the business of a song
To say who was right and who was wrong.

Both said the bitter things that pain
And wished they hadn't but said them again.

Till Carrie said at last one day:
'It's no use, Paul, I must go away.'

Paul struck a match and lit his pipe,
Said: 'It seems a pity but perhaps you're right.'

So Carrie returned to her home land,
Leading Tiny by the hand,

And Paul stayed in camp with his lumbermen,
Though he paid them visits now and then.

One day Tiny telegraphed him: 'Come quick.
Very worried. Mother sick.'

But the doctor met him at the door and said:
'I've bad news for you, Paul; she's dead.'

He ran upstairs and stood by the bed:
'Poor Carrie', he murmured and stroked her head.

'I know we fought and I was to blame
But I loved you greatly all the same.'

He picked up Tiny and stroked her hair,
Said: 'I've not been much of a father, dear.

'But I'll try to be better until the day
When you want to give your heart away.

'And whoever the lucky man may be,
I hope he's a better man than me.'

So they got ready to return
To the camp, of which you now shall learn.

Scene 2
The camp

LUMBERJACK 1: Nothing but soups and beans.
LUMBERJACK 2: Mondays, Wednesdays and Fridays soup.
LUMBERJACK 3: Tuesdays, Thursdays and Saturdays beans.
LUMBERJACK 1: Sundays, soup *and* beans.
LUMBERJACK 2: Soup gives me ulcers.

20

LUMBERJACK 3: I'm allergic to beans.

LUMBERJACK 1: Have you seen the chief about it, Johnny?

INKSLINGER: He's not back yet from his wife's funeral.

LUMBERJACK 2: Well, something's gotta be done about it, and done quick.

LUMBERJACK 3: You'll have to speak to them, yourself.

CHORUS of LUMBERJACKS: Things have gone too far.

No. 11 Food Chorus

CHORUS of LUMBERJACKS

Do I look the sort of fellow
Whom you might expect to bellow
    For a quail in aspic, or
Who would look as glum as Gandhi
If he wasn't offered brandy
    With a Lobster Thermidor?

Who would howl like some lost sinner
For a sherry before dinner,
    And demand a savoury;
Who would criticize the stuffing
In the olives, and drink nothing
    But Lapsang Suchong tea?

No, no, no, no.
Our digestion's pretty tough
And we're not particular,
But when they hand us out to eat
A lump of sandstone as the sweet,
Then things have gone too far.

Oh, the soup looks appetizing
Till you see a maggot rising
    White as Venus from the sea;
And a beetle in the cauli-
Flower isn't very jolly
    Or so it appears to me;

Flies have interesting features
And, of course they're all God's creatures,
    But a trifle out of place
In a glass of drinking water,
And it makes my temper shorter
    If I meet one face to face.

No, no, no, no.
Our digestion's pretty tough
And we're not particular,
But when we're even asked to crunch
A rat or cockroach with our lunch,
Then things have gone too far.

INKSLINGER

Iron, they say, is healthy,
And even wood is wealthy
    In essential vitamins;
But I hate to find a mallet
Tucked away in the fruit salad
    Or a hammer in the greens.

There are foods, so doctors tell you,
With a high nutritious value
    That the Middle Ages never knew;
But I can't secrete saliva
At the thought of a screwdriver
    Or a roasted walking shoe.

CHORUS of LUMBERJACKS

Our digestion's pretty tough
And we're not particular,
But when the kitchen offers one
A rusty thumb-tack underdone,
Then things have gone too far!

(*Enter* SAM SHARKEY *and* BEN BENNY.)

SAM SHARKEY and BEN BENNY: Anything wrong?

INKSLINGER: Please don't think for a moment we want to criticize. Your cooking's wonderful. We all know that Sam's soups are the finest in the world, and as for Ben's beans, why there isn't a dish like them anywhere. But don't you think that just occasionally, say once a month, we could have something different?

SAM SHARKEY: I can't believe it.

BEN BENNY: It's not possible.

SAM SHARKEY and BEN BENNY: After all we've done for them.

SAM SHARKEY: Haven't you stayed awake all night thinking how to please them?

BEN BENNY: Haven't you worked your fingers to the bone?

SAM SHARKEY: Day in, day out.

BEN BENNY: Week after week, month after month.

SAM SHARKEY: Year after year.

BEN BENNY: Not a word of thanks.

SAM SHARKEY: Just grumble, grumble, grumble.

BEN BENNY: Treating us like dogs.

SAM SHARKEY: I can't bear it any longer.

BEN BENNY: You don't know how much you've hurt us.

SAM SHARKEY: My nerves.

BEN BENNY: My art.

SAM SHARKEY and BEN BENNY: Very well. Very well. From now on you shall do the cooking yourselves.

INKSLINGER: Oh, but please. We didn't mean to upset you.

SAM SHARKEY: It's all right. We understand perfectly.

INKSLINGER: Sam. Ben. Please listen. I'm sorry if ...

BEN BENNY: Don't apologize. We're not angry.

SAM SHARKEY: Just a little sad, that's all.

BEN BENNY: One day perhaps you'll realize what you've done. Come, Sam.

SAM SHARKEY: Come, Ben.

(*Exeunt.*)

No. 12 Chorus Accusation

CROSS CROSSHAULSON
There now look what you have done.

INKSLINGER
What I did, you asked me to.

JEN JENSON
You know I only spoke in fun.

PETE PETERSON
I never understood what you
Meant to do.

ANDY ANDERSON
I said it wouldn't do,
You heard me, didn't you?

INKSLINGER
What would you have done instead?

CHORUS of LUMBERJACKS
Never mind. Beyond a doubt
You have put us in the red,
So you'd better get us out.

23

No. 12a Slim's Song

SLIM

(*Offstage.*)

In fair days and in foul
Round the world and back,
I must hunt my shadow
And the self I lack.

(SLIM *rides on.*)

INKSLINGER: Hullo, stranger. What's your name?
SLIM: Slim.
INKSLINGER: You don't look like a logger. Where do you come from?

SLIM

I come from open spaces
Where over endless grass
The stroking winds and shadows
Of cloud and bison pass;
My brothers were the buffalo,
My house the shining day,
I danced between the horse-hoofs like
A butterfly at play.

In fair days and in foul, etc.

One winter evening as I sat
By my camp fire alone,
I heard a whisper from the flame,
The voice was like my own:
'Oh get you up and get you gone,
North, South, or East or West,
This emptiness cannot answer
The heart in your breast.

'O ride till woods or houses
Provide the narrow place
Where you can force your fate to turn
And meet you face to face.'

In fair days and in foul
Round the world and back,
I must hunt my shadow
And the self I lack.

      FIDO, MOPPET and POPPET
    Ah!

INKSLINGER: Say, you can't cook by any chance?
SLIM: Sure.
CHORUS of LUMBERJACKS: Can you cook flapjacks?
SLIM: Yes.
CHORUS of LUMBERJACKS: Cookies?
SLIM: Yes.
CHORUS of LUMBERJACKS: Fish?
SLIM: Yes.
CHORUS of LUMBERJACKS: Steaks?
SLIM: Yes.
CHORUS of LUMBERJACKS: Are you telling lies?
SLIM: Yes. No. No. No.
CHORUS of LUMBERJACKS
You're an angel in disguise.
Sam and Benny get the sack.

No. 13 Bunyan's Return

CHORUS of LUMBERJACKS
Look, look the Chief is back.
And look, can I believe my eyes,
Is that a girl he's got with him?
Gosh, she's pretty and young and trim.
O boy.

(*Exeunt all but* FIDO *and* INKSLINGER.)

INKSLINGER: Hello, Fido. Staying to keep me company? That's mighty nice of you. Say, Fido, I want to ask you a question. Are you happy?

(FIDO *shakes his head.* INKSLINGER *goes to the door and looks to see if anyone is listening.*)

Then I'll tell you a secret. Neither am I, May I tell you the story of my life?

(FIDO *nods.*)

You're sure it won't bore you?

(FIDO *shakes his head but when* INKSLINGER *is not looking stifles a yawn with a paw.*)

No. 14 Inkslinger's Song

INKSLINGER

It was out in the sticks that the fire
    Of my existence began,
Where no one had heard the *Messiah*
    And no one had seen a Cézanne.
I learned a prose style from the preacher
    And the facts of life from the hens,
And fell in love with the teacher
    Whose love for John Keats was intense.
And I dreamed of writing a novel
    With which Tolstoy couldn't compete
And of how all the critics would grovel:
    But I guess that a guy gotta eat.

I can think of much nicer professions
    Than keeping a ledger correct,
Such as writing my private confessions
    Or procuring a frog to dissect.
Learning Sanskrit would be more amusing
    Or studying the history of Spain.
And, had I the power of choosing,
    I would live on the banks of the Seine.
I would paint St Sebastian the Martyr,
    Or dig up the Temples of Crete,
Or compose a D major Sonata:
    But I guess that a guy gotta eat.

The company I have to speak to
    Are wonderful men in their way,
But the things that delight me are Greek to
    The Jacks who haul lumber all day.
It isn't because I don't love them
    That this camp is a prison to me,
Nor do I think I'm above them
    In loathing the sight of a tree.
Oh, but where are those beautiful places
    Where what you begin you complete,
Where the joy shines out of men's faces,
    And all get sufficient to eat?

No. 14a Entrance of Chorus

PETE PETERSON
I never knew he had a daughter.

ANDY ANDERSON
She's much lovelier than I thought her.

JEN JENSON
Tiny, what a pretty name.

CROSS CROSSHAULSON
I am delighted that she came.

PETE PETERSON
Her eyes,

JEN JENSON
Her cheeks,

CROSS CROSSHAULSON
Her lips,

ANDY ANDERSON
Her nose.

JEN JENSON
She's a peach,

JOHN SHEARS
A dove,

PETE PETERSON
A rose.

(*Enter* TINY.)

No. 15 Tiny's Entrance

BEN BENNY: Look at me, Miss Tiny: I'm six feet tall.

SAM SHARKEY: Look at me, Miss Tiny: I've the bluest eyes you ever saw.

CROSS CROSSHAULSON: Feel my biceps, Miss Tiny.

ANDY ANDERSON: I can ride a bicycle.

JOHN SHEARS: I can spell parallelogram.

ANDY ANDERSON: I've got fifty dollars salted away in an old sock.

JOHN SHEARS: I'll run errands for you.

SAM SHARKEY: I'll bring your breakfast in bed.

BEN BENNY: I'll tell you stories before you go to sleep.

ANDY ANDERSON: I'll make you laugh by pulling faces.

BEN BENNY: I'm big and husky. You need someone to look after you.

JOHN SHEARS: You need someone to look after; I'm sick.

No. 15a Tiny's Song

TINY

Ah!

INKSLINGER: Leave her alone, you fools. Have you forgotten her mother's just died?

TINY

Ah!
Whether the sun shines upon children playing,
Or storms endanger the sailors at sea,
In a solitude or a conversation,
Mother, O Mother, tears arise in me.

For underground now you rest who at nightfall
Would sing me to sleep in my little bed;
I turn with the world but grief has no motion;
Mother, O Mother, too soon you were dead.

O never again in fatigue or fever
Shall I feel your cool hand upon my brow;
As you look after the cherubs in Heaven,
Mother, O Mother, look down on me now.

Should a day come I hear a lover whisper,
Should I stay an old maid whom the men pass by,
My heart shall cherish your guardian image,
Mother, O Mother, till the day I die.

CHORUS of LUMBERJACKS

The white bone
Lies alone
Like the limestone
Under the green grass.
All time goes by;
We too shall lie
Under death's eye.
Alas, alas.

TINY

Alas.

(*Enter* SLIM.)

SLIM: Supper's ready.
TINY: Excuse me, are you the cook?
SLIM: Yes, mam.
TINY: I'm Miss Tiny. Father said I was to help you in the kitchen.
SLIM: I'm sure you'll be a great help, Miss Tiny. This way, please.

(*As they exeunt:*)

LUMBERJACK 1: Did you see how he looked at her?
LUMBERJACK 2: Did you see how she looked at him?
LUMBERJACK 3: I shall take cooking lessons.
Rest of CHORUS of LUMBERJACKS: Don't chatter so. Let's go and eat.

(*Exeunt.*)

No. 16 Inkslinger's Regret
INKSLINGER

(*Alone.*)

All the little brooks of love
    Run down towards each other.
Somewhere every valley ends,
    And loneliness is over.
Some meet early, some meet late,
    Some, like me, have long to wait.

VOICE of PAUL BUNYAN: Johnny.
INKSLINGER: Yes, Mr Bunyan.
VOICE of PAUL BUNYAN: Has anything happened since I've been away?
INKSLINGER: Keep an eye on Hel Helson. He broods too much by himself and I don't like the look on his face. And the bunch he goes around with are a bad bunch.
VOICE of PAUL BUNYAN: Poor Hel. He was born a few hundred years too late. Today there is no place for him. Anything else?
INKSLINGER: Some of the men say they are tired of logging and would like to settle down. They'd like to try farming.
VOICE of PAUL BUNYAN: John Shears?
INKSLINGER: He's the chief one but there are many others.
VOICE of PAUL BUNYAN: I'll look into it. And what about yourself, Johnny?
INKSLINGER: I'm all right, Mr Bunyan.
VOICE of PAUL BUNYAN: I know what you want. It's harder than you think and not so pleasant. But you shall have it and shan't have to wait much longer. Good night, Johnny.
INKSLINGER: Good night, Mr Bunyan.
VOICE of PAUL BUNYAN: Still *Mr* Bunyan?
INKSLINGER: Good night, Paul.

(*Exit* INKSLINGER.)

CHORUS of LUMBERJACKS: (*Offstage*) Good night, Mr Bunyan.
VOICE of PAUL BUNYAN: Good night. Happy dreams.

No. 17 Bunyan's Goodnight (iii)

VOICE of PAUL BUNYAN
Now let the complex spirit dissolve in the darkness
Where the Actual and the Possible are mysteriously exchanged.
For the saint must descend into Hell; that his order may be tested by its disorder,
The hero return to the humble womb; that his will may be pacified and refreshed.
Dear children, trust the night and have faith in tomorrow,
That these hours of ambiguity and indecision may be also the hours of healing.

ACT TWO

Scene 1
A clearing in the forest

No. 18 Bunyan's Good Morning

VOICE of PAUL BUNYAN
The songs of dawn have been sung and the night watchmen are already in the deep
 beginnings of sleep.

Leaning upon their implements the hired men pause to consider their life by the
 light of mid-morning, and of habits already established in their loosened limbs.
And the aggressive will is no longer pure.

Much has been done to prepare a continent for the rejoicings and recriminations of
 all its possible heirs.
Much has been ill done. There is never enough time to do more than one thing at a
 time, and there is always either too much of one thing or too little.

Virtuosos of the axe, dynamiters and huntsmen, there has been an excess of military
 qualities, of the resourcefulness of thieves, the camaraderie of the irresponsible,
 and the accidental beauties of silly songs.

Nevertheless you have done much to render yourselves unnecessary.
Loneliness has worn lines of communication.
Irrational destruction has made possible the establishment of a civilized order.
Drunkenness and lechery have prepared the way for a routine of temperance and
 marriage.
Already you have provoked a general impulse towards settlement and cultivation.

(*Enter* CHORUS of LUMBERJACKS.)

CHORUS of LUMBERJACKS
What does he want to see us for?
I wonder what he has in store.
I never did a thing I shouldn't,
I couldn't. I wouldn't.
I'll do my work. I'll never shirk.
I'll never never grumble any more.

VOICE of PAUL BUNYAN: I've been thinking for some time that we needed some
  farmers to grow food for the camp, and looking around for a nice piece of
  country, the other day I found the very place. A land where the wheat grows as
  tall as churches and the potatoes are as big as airships. Now those who would
  like to be farmers: Stand out.

No. 18a Shears's Song

JOHN SHEARS
It has always been my dream
  Since I was only so high
To live upon a farm and watch
  The wheat and barley grow high.

CHORUS of FARMERS
The wheat and barley grow high.

VOICE of PAUL BUNYAN: Hel Helson.
HEL HELSON: Yes.
VOICE of PAUL BUNYAN: You are in charge while I take our friends to the land of
  Heart's Desire. I want you to start today clearing the Topsy Turvey Mountain.
  Now boys, if you're ready we'll start as we have a thousand miles to go before
  noon. But if you think farming is a soft job you'd better stay right here.

No. 18b Bunyan's Warning

VOICE of PAUL BUNYAN
If there isn't a flood, there's a drought.
If there isn't a frost, there's a heatwave.
If it isn't the insects, it's the banks.
You'll howl more than you'll sing,
You'll frown more than you'll smile,
You'll cry more than you'll laugh.
But some people seem to like it.
Let's get going.

No. 19 Farmers' Song

JOHN SHEARS

The shanty-boy invades the wood
Upon his cruel mission
To slay the tallest trees he can
The height of his ambition.

FARMER 2

The farmer heeds wild Nature's cry
For Higher Education,
And is a trusted friend to all
The best in vegetation.

CHORUS of FARMERS

I hate to be a shanty-boy,
I want to be a farmer,
For I prefer life's comedy
To life's crude melodrama.

JOHN SHEARS

The shanty-boy sleeps in a bunk
With none to call him Dad, sir,
And so you cannot wonder much
If he goes to the bad, sir.

FARMER 2

The farmer sees his little ones
Grow up like the green willow.
At night he has his Better Half
Beside him on the pillow.

CHORUS of FARMERS

I hate to be a shanty-boy,
I want to be a farmer,
For I prefer life's comedy
To life's crude melodrama.

No. 19a Farmers' Exit

(*The others watch them go and all except* HEL HELSON *and his* FOUR CRONIES *exeunt.*)

CRONY 1: The Topsy Turvey Mountain. It's impossible.
CRONY 2: He's nuts.
CRONY 3: Just another of his crazy ideas.
CRONY 4: You are not going to take him seriously, are you, Hel?
CRONY 1: Why do you go on taking orders from a dope like that?

CRONY 2: Why don't you run this joint yourself? We'd support you.
CRONY 3: Sure we would.
CRONY 4: Hel for Boss.
CRONY 1: Tell him where he gets off.
CRONY 2: And that stooge of his, Johnny Inkslinger.
CRONY 3: You said it. We'll take him for a ride.
CRONY 4: Stand up for your rights, Hel. You're the only boss around here.
HEL HELSON: Get out.
CRONY 1: Of course, Hel.
CRONY 2: Anything you say, boss.
CRONY 3: We were just going anyway.
CRONY 4: Don't forget what we think of you.

(*Exeunt* FOUR CRONIES. HELSON *is left sitting moodily alone.*)

No. 20 The Mocking of Hel Helson

HEL HELSON
Heron, heron winging by
Through the silence of the sky,
What have you heard of me, Helson the Brave?

HERON
Oh, I heard of a hero working for wages,
Taking orders just like a slave.

CHORUS
No! I'm afraid it's too late,
Helson never will be great.

HEL HELSON
Moon, moon shining bright
In the deserts of the night,
What have you heard of Helson the Fair?

MOON
Not what one should hear of one so handsome,
The girls make fun of his bashful air.

CHORUS
No! I'm afraid it's too late,
Helson never will be great.

33

HEL HELSON
Wind, wind as you run
Round and round the earth for fun,
What have you heard of Helson the Good?

WIND
Oh, the old story of virtue neglected,
Mocked at by others, misunderstood.

CHORUS
No! I'm afraid it's too late,
Helson never will be great.

HEL HELSON
Beetle! Beetle! Squirrel! Squirrel!
Beetle, as you pass
Down the avenues of grass,
Squirrel, as you go
Through the forests to and fro,
What have you heard of Helson the Wise? of Helson the Strong?

BEETLE
It's sad to think of all that wisdom
Being exploited by smarter guys.

SQUIRREL
Not what one likes to hear of a fighter,
They say he's a coward, I hope they're wrong.

CHORUS
Too late! Too late! Too late!
He will never, never, never be great!

(*Enter* FIDO, MOPPET *and* POPPET.)

MOPPET: Did you really?
POPPET: Yes, I says, excuse me, I says, but this is my roof, what of it, he says, you're
trespassing, I says, and if I am, he says, who's going to stop me, yours truly, I
says, scram alley cat, he says, before I eat you, I don't know about alley cats, I
says, but one doesn't need to be a detective to see who has a rat in his family
tree, and the fight was on.
FIDO: There now, just look. Helson has got the blues again. Dear O dear, that man
has the worst inferiority complexes I've ever run across. His dreams must be
amazing. Really I must ask him about them. Excuse me.
MOPPET: Nosy prig.
POPPET: He can't help it. Dogs are like that. Always sniffing.

34

No. 21 Fido's Sympathy

FIDO

(*Looking up at* HELSON.)

Won't you tell me what's the matter?
I adore the confidential role,
Why not tell your little troubles
To a really sympathetic soul?

(HELSON *lunges a kick at him and he bolts.*)

POPPET: Dogs have no *savoir-faire*.
MOPPET: Serve him right. I hate gush.

No. 22 Cats' Creed

MOPPET and POPPET

Let Man the romantic in vision espy
A far better world than his own in the sky
As a tyrant or beauty express a vain wish
To be mild as a beaver or chaste as a fish.

Let the dog who's the most sentimental of all
Throw a languishing glance at the hat in the hall,
Struggle wildly to speak all the tongues that he hears
And to rise to the realm of Platonic ideas.

But the cat is an Aristotelian and proud
Preferring hard fact to intangible cloud;
Like the Troll in Peer Gynt, both in hunting and love,
The cat has one creed: 'To thyself be enough!'

POPPET: Let's go and kill birds.
MOPPET: You've heard about Tiny and Slim? Fido caught them necking in the
pantry after breakfast.
POPPET: Yes, he told me. No one can say I'm narrow-minded, but there are *some*
things that just aren't done till after dark.

(*Exeunt.*)

VOICE of PAUL BUNYAN: Helson, Helson.

(*Enter* FOUR CRONIES.)

CRONY 1: He's back.
CRONY 2: He's mad at you.
VOICE of PAUL BUNYAN: Helson, I want to talk to you.
CRONY 3: Don't pay any attention to him.

CRONY 4: Go and settle with him.
VOICE of PAUL BUNYAN: Helson.
CRONY 1: You're not going to do what he tells you, are you?
CRONY 2: Go on, wipe the floor with him.
CRONY 3: Don't let him think you're sissy.
CRONY 4: Show him you're an American. Give him the works.
HEL HELSON: I'll kill him.

(*Exit* HELSON.)

FOUR CRONIES: Atta boy.

No. 23 The Fight

(CHORUS *rush in.*)

CHORUS

What's happening?
What is it?
A fight!
It's Helson!
He's crazy!
He'll kill him!
They're heaving rocks!
That's got him!
No, missed him!
Gosh! did you see that?
Helson is tough!
But Paul has the brains.

(*They stream out to watch the fight. Enter* SLIM *and* TINY.)

Love Duet

TINY: Slim.
SLIM: Yes, dear.
TINY: Where has everybody gone?
SLIM: I don't know, but I'm glad.
TINY: Darling.

(*They embrace. Thunder and shouts off.*)

SLIM

Move, move from the trysting stone,
White sun of summer depart.

36

That I may be left alone
With my true love close to my heart.

(*Thunder and shouts off.*)

SLIM: Tiny.
TINY: Yes, dear.
SLIM: Did you hear a funny noise?
TINY: I did, but I don't care.
SLIM: Darling.

(*They embrace.*)

TINY
The head that I love the best

SLIM
Shall lie all night on my breast.

CHORUS
(*Offstage.*)

Paul! Helson!
Helson is tough!
But Paul has the brains!

TINY: Slim.
SLIM: Yes, dear.
TINY: How do people really know they really are in love?
TINY and SLIM: Darling.

TINY and SLIM
Lost, lost is the world I knew,
And I have lost myself too;
Dear heart, I am lost in you.

CHORUS
(*Offstage.*)

He's got him! Now!

(*Enter* CHORUS *carrying the unconscious body of* HEL HELSON.)

Mock Funeral March

CHORUS

Take away the body and lay it on the ice,
Put a lily in his hand and beef-steaks on his eyes;
Twenty tall white candles at his feet and head;
And let this epitaph be read:

Here lies an unlucky picayune;
He thought he was champ but he thought too soon.
Here lies Hel Helson from Scandinavia,
Rather regretting his rash behaviour.

CRONY 1

We told him not to,
We never forgot to.

CRONY 2

Be careful to say
He should obey.

CRONY 3

'Helson,' we said,
'Get this in your head,

CRONY 4

'Take orders from Paul
Or you'll have a fall.'

CRONIES 1 and 2

We are all put here on earth for a purpose. We all have a job to do and it is our duty to do it with all our might.

CRONIES 3 and 4

We must obey our superiors and live according to our station in life; for whatever the circumstances, the Chief, the Company and the Customer are always right.

HEL HELSON

Where am I? What happened? Am I dead?
Something struck me on the head.

CHORUS

It's all right, Hel, you're not dead,
You are lying in your bed.

HEL HELSON

Why am I so stiff and sore?
I remember nothing more.

38

All right, Hel, don't be a sap,
You'd a kind of little scrap;
Don't worry now but take a nap.

HEL HELSON
Who was it hit me on the chin?

VOICE of PAUL BUNYAN
I'm sorry, Hel, I had to do it.
I'm your friend, if you but knew it.

HEL HELSON
Good Heavens! What a fool I've been!

VOICE of PAUL BUNYAN
Let bygones be bygones. Forget the past.
We can now be friends at last.
Each of us has found a brother.
You and I both need each other.

FOUR CRONIES
That's what we always told you, Hel.

HEL HELSON
How could I ever have been so blind
As not to recognize your kind.
Now I know you. Scram. Or else.

CHORUS
Scram. Or else.

FOUR CRONIES
Ingratitude!
A purely selfish attitude!
An inability to see a joke
And characteristic of uneducated folk.

CHORUS
Scram. Or else.

FOUR CRONIES
Don't argue with them. They're sick people.

CHORUS
Scram, or else!

(*Exeunt* CRONIES.)

Hymn

Often thoughts of hate conceal
Love we are ashamed to feel;
In the climax of a fight
Lost affection comes to light.

CHORUS with HELSON

And the prisoners are set free
O great day of discovery!

TINY and SLIM

Move, move from the trysting stone,
White sun of summer depart.
That I may be left alone
With my true love close to my heart.

TINY, SLIM and CHORUS

The head that I love the best
Shall lie all night on my breast.
Lost, lost is the world I knew,
And I am lost, dear heart, in you!

HEL HELSON

Great day of discovery!

CHORUS

Great day!

No. 24 Third Ballad Interlude

NARRATOR

So Helson smiled and Bunyan smiled
And both shook hands and were reconciled.

And Paul and Johnny and Hel became
The greatest partners in the logging game.

And every day Slim and Tiny swore
They were more in love than the day before.

All over the States the stories spread
Of Bunyan's camp and the life they led.

Of fights with Indians, of shooting matches,
Of monster bears and salmon catches.

40

Of the whirling whimpus Paul fought and killed,
Of the Buttermilk Line that he had to build.

And a hundred other tales were known
From Nantucket Island to Oregon.

From the Yiddish Alps to the Rio Grande,
From the Dust Bowl down to the Cotton Land.

In every dialect and tongue
His tales were told and his stories sung,

Harsh in the Bronx where they cheer with zest,
With a burring R in the Middle West,

And lilting and slow in Arkansas
Where instead of Father they say Paw.

But there came a winter, these stories say,
When Babe came up to Paul one day,

Stood still and looked him in the eye;
Paul said nothing for he knew why.

'Shoulder your axe and leave this place:
Let the clerk move in with his well-washed face.

'Let the architect with his sober plan
Build a residence for the average man;

'And garden birds not bat an eye
When locomotives whistle by;

'And telephone wires go from town to town
For lovers to whisper sweet nothings down. †

'We must depart – but it's Christmas Eve –
So let's have a feast before we leave.'

That is all I have to tell,
The party's starting; friends, farewell.

† Optional cut

41

Scene 2

No. 25 The Christmas Party

(*Christmas Eve. A full-size pine-tree lit up as a Christmas tree in background. Foreground a big table with candles.* CHORUS *eating dinner. Funny hats, streamers, noises.*)

CHORUS

Another slice of turkey, another slice of ham,
I'll feel sick to-morrow, but I don't give a damn.
Take a quart of whiskey and mix it with your beer,
Pass the gravy, will you? Christmas comes but once a year.

FIDO

Men are three parts crazy and no doubt always were,
But why do they go mad completely one day in the year?

CHORUS

Who wants the Pope's nose? I do.
French fried if you please,
I've a weakness for plum pudding.
Would you pass the cheese?
Wash it down with Bourbon.
I think I'll stick to Rye.
There's nothing to compare with real old-fashioned pie.

MOPPET and POPPET

Seeing his temper's so uncertain, it's very queer,
He should always be good-tempered one day in the year.

CHORUS

Cigars!
Hurrah!
Some nuts!
I'm stuffed to here!
Your health!
Skol!
Prosit!
Santé!
Cheers!
A merry, merry Christmas and a happy New Year.

(INKSLINGER *bangs on the table and rises.*)

INKSLINGER

Dear friends, with your leave this Christmas Eve
    I rise to make a pronouncement;
Some will have guessed but I thought it best
    To make an official announcement.

Hot Biscuit Slim, you all know him,
    As your cook (or *coquus* in Latin)
Has been put in charge of a very large
    Hotel in Mid-Manhattan.

(*Cheers.*)

But Miss Tiny here, whom we love so dear,
    I understand has now consented
To share his life as his loving wife.
    They both look very contented.

THREE SOLOS from CHORUS

Carry her over the water,
    Set her down under the tree,
Where the culvers white all day and all night,
    And the winds from every quarter,
Sing agreeably, agreeably, agreeably of love.

FIDO, MOPPET and POPPET

Put a gold ring on her finger,
    Press her close to your heart,
While the fish in the lake their snapshots take,
    And the frog, that sanguine singer,
Sings agreeably, agreeably, agreeably of love.

CHORUS

The preacher shall dance at your marriage,
    The steeple bend down to look,
The pulpit and chairs shed suitable tears,
    While the horses drawing your carriage
Sing agreeably, agreeably, agreeably of love.

TINY and SLIM

(*Rising.*)

Where we are is not very far
    To walk from Grand Central Station,
If you ever come East, you will know at least
    Of a standing invitation.

(They sit down.)

INKSLINGER

And Hel so tall who managed for Paul
And had the task of converting
His ambitious dreams into practical schemes
And of seeing we all were working,

Will soon be gone to Washington
To join the Administration
As a leading man in the Federal Plan
Of public works for the nation.

(Cheers. HELSON *rises.)*

HEL HELSON

I hope that some of you will come
To offer your assistance
In installing turbines and High Tension lines
And bringing streams from a distance.

(Cheers. He sits down.)

INKSLINGER

And now three cheers for old John Shears
Who has taken a short vacation
From his cattle and hay, to be with us today
On this important occasion.

(Cheers. JOHN SHEARS *rises.)*

JOHN SHEARS

(Stammering.)

I am ... I'm not ... er which, er what ...
As I was saying ... the er ...
The er ... the well, I mean, O Hell,
I'm mighty glad to be here.

(Cheers. He sits down.)

WESTERN UNION BOY

(Offstage.)

Inkslinger! John Inkslinger!

(Enter WESTERN UNION BOY, *on his bicycle.)*

44

A telegram, a telegram,
A telegram from Hollywood.
Inkslinger is the name;
And I think that the news is good.

INKSLINGER: (*Reading*) 'Technical Adviser required for all-star lumber picture stop
your name suggested stop if interested wire collect stop.'

A lucky break, am I awake?
Please pinch me if I'm sleeping.
It only shows that no one knows
The future of bookkeeping.

CHORUS

We always knew that one day you
Would come to be famous, Johnny.
When you're prosperous remember us
And we'll all sing Hey Nonny, Nonny.

INKSLINGER

And last of all I call on Paul
To speak to us this evening,
I needn't say how sad today
We are that he is leaving.

Every eye is ready to cry
At the thought of bidding adieu, sir,
For sad is the heart when friends must part,
But enough – I call upon you, sir.

No. 26 Bunyan's Farewell

VOICE of PAUL BUNYAN
Now the task that made us friends
In a common labour, ends;
For an emptiness is named
And a wilderness is tamed
Till its savage nature can
Tolerate the life of man.

All I had to do is done,
You remain but I go on;
Other kinds of deserts call,
Other forests whisper Paul;
I must hasten to reply
To that low instinctive cry,

There to make a way again
For the conscious lives of men.

Here, though, is your life, and here
The pattern is already clear
That machinery imposes
On you as the frontier closes,
Gone the natural disciplines
And the life of choice begins.

You and I must go our way;
I have but one word to say:
O remember, friends, that you
Have the harder task to do
As at freedom's puzzled feet
Yawn the gulfs of self-defeat;
All but heroes are unnerved
When life and love must be deserved.

No. 27 Litany

CHORUS
The campfire embers are black and cold,
The banjos are broken, the stories are told,
The woods are cut down, and the young grown old.

FIDO, MOPPET and POPPET
From a Pressure Group that says I am the Constitution,
From those who say Patriotism and mean Persecution,
From a Tolerance that is really inertia and disillusion:

CHORUS
Save animals and men.

TINY and SLIM: Bless us, father.
VOICE of PAUL BUNYAN
A father cannot bless.
May you find the happiness that you possess.

CHORUS
The echoing axe shall be heard no more
Nor the rising scream of the buzzer saw
Nor the crash as the ice-jam explodes in the thaw.

FIDO, MOPPET and POPPET
From entertainments neither true nor beautiful nor witty,
From a homespun humour manufactured in the city,
From the dirty-mindedness of a Watch Committee:

CHORUS
Save animals and men.

HEL HELSON: Don't leave us, Paul. What's to become of America now?
VOICE of PAUL BUNYAN
Every day America's destroyed and re-created,
America is what you do,
America is I and you,
America is what you choose to make it.

CHORUS
No longer the logger shall hear in the Fall
The pine and the spruce and the sycamore call.

VOICE of PAUL BUNYAN: Goodbye, dear friends.

CHORUS
Goodbye, Paul.

FIDO, MOPPET and POPPET
From children brought up to believe in self-expression,
From the theology of plumbers or the medical profession,
From depending on alcohol for self-respect and self-possession:

CHORUS
Save animals and men.

INKSLINGER: Paul, who are you?
VOICE of PAUL BUNYAN
Where the night becomes the day,
Where the dream becomes the fact,
I am the Eternal Guest,
I am Way,
I am Act.

END